P G Holroyd

GreenBeard's Vegan Verse

By

P G Holroyd

P G Holroyd

I dedicate this, my first book, to my beautiful
vegan offspring,

Thomas and Annie

Also, to all the activists who are, or have been protesting at
CAMP BEAGLE (U.K.)
This was the first poem I wrote...

Close down MBR Acres

Thousands of puppies a year are bred
To go to laboratories and end up dead
Their mothers are used again and again
To produce more babies for heartless men

Trained to accept injections and masks
The puppies comply and do as they're asked
Their trust is betrayed with poison instead
To see how long they will last 'til they're dead

These pointless experiments on innocent souls
Should not be allowed, let's make it our goal
To free all the Beagles from hands of blood
And shut down MBR Acres for good!

P G Holroyd

Welcome to GreenBeard's Vegan Verse

GreenBeard is the name I use for my animal rights poems, and make no mistake, these poems are a form of activism. I find I can't write about the subject of animal rights and the awful conditions most of them are subjected to without getting angry and frustrated*, which is not my usual demeanour, so *GreenBeard* steps in.

*(angry and frustrated mostly at myself for not seeing it sooner, when I call out non-vegans in these poems I'm also aiming it at my former self)

I hope you enjoy this collection of poems, despite the subject, and that they can help in some way to get a point across on behalf of the billions of oppressed animals in the world, either by way of reciting them at an event or to a family member, or if you yourself are wondering why you should care.
I have tried to make the verse easy to read and memorise, and to get straight to the point.
No long, clever, and sophisticated poetry from me.

GreenBeard doesn't beat about the bush, he wears it as a beard!

P G Holroyd

Contents

P G Holroyd

1   POEM FOR THE ANIMALS
All of them!

POEM FOR THE ANIMALS

Roses are red, blood is too,
animals are dead because of you
If you wear them, you ended their life,
if you eat them, you wielded the knife
When you drink their milk they die, there's no maybe,
you're stealing the food they made for their baby

Factory farming, tortured from birth,
for you it's a sandwich, for them, *Hell on Earth*
When you buy your eggs, think of the cost,
billions of chickens whose lives have been lost
And what of the male chicks, unable to lay,
mass-murdered in grinders and just thrown away

Innocent beings, horribly mutilated,
animal testing is barbaric and dated
Some say it's natural to ride a horse round a track,
but it's not *natural anatomy* to have a
prick on your back
Hunting is murder, whether hound, bow or gun,
if they were the hunted would it still be such fun?

Humans are the monsters to some of this Earth, but
we don't have to be evil, can you measure your worth?
We can *eat without killing,* leave animals alone,
there's so much choice, *all our food can be grown*

There'd be plenty of food without livestock to feed,
for the starving people who are always in need
There's no need to breed them, just let them live,
and see all the joy and the love they can give

2   HUMANE SLAUGHTER
No such thing

Humane Slaughter

Tell me again how you think it's humane for an animal's throat to be cut

Tell me again that they're feeling no pain as they're bleeding out hung by one foot

From the fear in their eyes to their terrified cries you can see that

they all want to live

They're tortured and raped with no chance of escape,

"It's humane" is the answer you give?

Humane you will find, means **caring** and **kind**, for the *victims*

those words don't exist

Cruelty and **death** are all they have left of their lives as the slaughter persists

The process is led with a *bolt to the head*, then a *knife to the throat* to be sure

Before they are dead, they'll *cut off their head,*

all those workers like rats in a sewer

Sometimes *pigs are gassed* by a poisonous blast of **carbon dioxide** in cages

The poor pigs will squeal as they all start to feel the effects, and

it goes on for ages

After *dying in fits* they're *cut into bits* and some people will see that as food

And though it's labelled as *'fresh'* it's just rotting *flesh*

to be selfishly tasted and chewed

I just don't know why someone would apply for a job killing innocent souls

Some kind of **fool** or **sadistic** and **cruel**, are they really achieving their goals?

Maybe they're proud to be part of the crowd who enjoy causing **terror** and **pain**

But don't take the piss and tell me that this

is in any way *fucking humane!*

3   A PIGS LIFE
Very short and BRUTAL!

A PIG'S LIFE

Born five months ago a litter of ten start life in prison cells
Created to feed the hunger of men, three boys and seven girls
All feeding from their mother's teats, *they never see her face*
She's held down in a tiny cage,
in that nightmare of a place

Scared and alone they try to stay alive,
the strongest gaining weight
No more room for the smallest to survive, so
ten babies become eight

Five months old
and it's time to go on their one and only outing
Packed in tight with hundreds more
forced in with kicks and shouting
Now they're on the move the siblings see the outside world
Maybe going to a better place? these lucky boys and girls
But no, the final destination proves to be much worse
Unloaded at the slaughterhouse
they can't escape their curse

Born five months ago,
a litter of eight end life on the killing floor
Destined to be the food of men*, in pieces, in the store*

4   VIGIL

Activists showing respect and saying goodbye to the
animals about to be slaughtered

VIGIL

We're here to bear witness to you, the *condemned*
Soon to be *murdered* by ruthless men
And though it won't help you to have us here
Please know that we're grieving and shedding a tear

Your miserable life was spent on *death row*
Unable to move and with nowhere to go
And what was your crime that brings you here now?
You were born a *pig, sheep, chicken* or *cow*

You arrive by the *thousands* in trucks every day
A nightmare of a journey in every way
You've been taken from the *Hellhole* that was your life
And brought to a new *Hell* and the butcher's knife

The lorry will take you far out of our sight
But we'll still hear your *screams* well into the night
As you wait in line for your turn to be *killed*
And *you're watching it happen*, and the fridges are filled

Now the truck drives out empty, and another arrives
More *meat* for the masses, *more innocent lives*
And the most we can do is just watch you in vain
Ashamed to be human, full of heartache and pain

We're here to bear witness to you, the *condemned*
And we'll keep on coming 'til this *holocaust* ends
Until the law recognises that *all animals' lives*
Are worth more than a sandwich to be sliced up with knives

5   BRED FOR EGGS

Organic, 'free-range', it's all the same, disgusting

BRED FOR EGGS

A *new life* hatches from a broken shell, a baby bird pops out
Full of wonder in a brand-new world, but their future is in doubt
No chance to meet his mother, this poor chick was born a male
So along with all his brothers, *life becomes an instant fail*
Thrown onto conveyor belts, a real-life road to *Hell*
The babies travel to their death, just a day out of their shell
Ground-up alive or *bagged and gassed*, regarded as mere dregs
The destiny of millions *just because they can't lay eggs*

The sisters of these ill-fated souls have longer lives to live
Thrown into barn or cage for all the *eggs they have to give*
A fraction of their natural life the chickens barely last a year
With bodies broken and feathers gone the slaughterhouse draws near
Bred to lay, day after day, the poor girls cannot cope
Treated like machinery there isn't any hope
So when they're spent, can't pay the rent with nothing left to give
They pay with flesh, though far from fresh, with no more life to live

Such is the state, and the terrible fate of *chickens bred for eggs*
Until they quit, then throats are slit and hung up by their legs
And all because the life that was the same as all on Earth
Provides a snack, a child's lunch-pack,
that's all their lives are worth
You might not care, might even dare to laugh at such a thing
They're only birds, and so these words are never gonna sting
But they feel pain, so think again, if it was done to you
How would it feel to be a meal, you haven't got a clue

6 POULTRY POETRY

All those birds living in HELL and we're the Demons

Poultry Poetry

Just a few weeks old and you have them for dinner
Does that make you feel proud, *do you feel like a winner?*
These helpless babies have just been born
And in just a few weeks their bodies are worn
Fattened so quickly they outgrow their legs
Unable to stand, *bred for meat*, not for eggs
Then turned into burgers and nuggets and things
And *you gorge on their bodies*, their legs and their wings

Chickens and **turkeys** and **ducks** and **geese**
You suck on their bones, all covered in grease
Their feed funnelled in as if fuelling a truck
And you eat the same way *'cause you don't give a fuck*
Their overstuffed bodies make them look fully grown
Their lives just begun, and to slaughter they're thrown
You call it a *feast* and give thanks for your meal
But *those lives weren't given*, the true word is *steal*

You say it's up to you, what you eat is your choice
But what would they choose if they had a voice?
They're sentient beings, they can *feel*, they can *think*
And we reduce them to scraps to be washed down the sink
You see them as *something*, not the *someone* they are
Some inanimate object, like a bike or a car
If we could see through their eyes do you know what we'd find?
Monsters do exist in this world, and they're called *Mankind*

7 DAIRY KILLS

Not your mum, not your milk

Dairy Kills

Ever wondered how so much milk is supplied?
For so many *billions* of people worldwide
They tell you it's *natural* and *fortified*,
but it's a long way from nature, ***the truth is they lied***

It starts with them *masturbating the bull*,
then an arm up the cow by way of anal
Injecting semen until the cervix is full,
what part of this violation can be called natural?

Nine months later the calf is born, and the milk is produced,
but the baby is torn
Away from the mother, alone and forlorn
so the milk can be sold, *and the cycle goes on*

The ***male calves are killed*** as they aren't any use,
the females destined for a ***life of abuse***
The mothers are *heartbroken*, what's the excuse?
Because we like the taste of the things they produce

In just a few years the mothers are spent, a few years of
anguish, pain and ***torment***
Then off to the same place that their mothers went, a new
kind of *Hell*, ***to the slaughter they're sent***

This is the cost of **milk, butter** and **cheese**, the
dairy cows living their lives on their knees
But we can change it, and we can do it with ease,
when you go shopping. ***choose an alternative,***
PLEASE!

8 MILK

We don't need it, the baby does

Milk

When a tiger has cubs she feeds them her milk,
that's what she produces it for
The same goes for mammals all over the world,
the mother gives birth, the milk starts to pour

The puppies drink milk from the dog,
the foal drinks milk from the horse
Piglets drink milk from the pig, and kittens from the cat of course
Baby elephants drink milk from their mothers,
the lamb drinks milk from the ewe
The monkey provides milk for her infant,

and the cow gives her milk to...*what?...* ***you?***

Humans are mammals, the same as the rest,
the mother provides milk for her baby
So why do we need to steal from the calf,
Is there something wrong with that maybe?
Of all the mammals, all over the world,
whose babies drink milk from their mum
Only humans drink baby milk their whole adult lives
from another ***species***, that's what we've become

Don't you think that's a little bit dumb?
Do you think that the cow is your mum?

The only right way, when sanity comes,
is to let the calves feed from their mums!

9   ADOPT, DON'T SHOP

Rehome an orphan, don't pay to make more

Adopt, Don't Shop

How much is that doggy in the window?
The one with the waggly tail
The true cost of that pup would make you throw up
It's much more than the price of the sale

The doggy in that window cost heartache and pain
His mum forced to give birth again and again
Until the day she's used up, too tired for more pups
Then she's thrown away or brutally slain

That mother was stolen, or her mother was
And so was the father, they steal them because
Some people will pay a high price to say
That "My dog's a 'pure bred' is yours?"

The puppies are farmed in large numbers you see
And *caged up in squalor and misery*
Until they are sold for maximum gold
To *ignorant people* too blind to see

The breeders will profit while there's the demand
Puppy farms spreading all over the land
So rescue, don't shop, it's best to adopt
They're individuals, not just a brand

So many animals in need of a home
Waiting for someone who loves them to come
To be their best friend right up to the end
And see how much richer both lives can become

10   VIVISECTION

If it's tested on animals, DON'T BUY IT!

Vivisection

We humans have a new disease, what are we to do?
Let's **take another species** and give it to them too
Will that help to cure us? We haven't got a clue,
But it gives sadistic scientists a job they like to do

Inject it in an animal, try the monkeys first
If it doesn't kill them keep injecting 'til they burst
It's not affecting them so much, in us it gets much worse
Lucky them! Let's cut them up and open like a purse

This new brand of cigarettes means there's tests we have to do
Let's use the rabbits over there, **the ones blinded by shampoo**
Keep pumping smoke into their lungs and watch their skin turn blue
And if they die, the dogs we'll try, to get this product through

Put those mice in water, and **leave them 'til they drown**
This monkey won't stop struggling, someone help me **hold her down**
Be sure to monitor the heart rate while they're **thrashing all around**
I'm hungry now, let's go to lunch, it's **happy hour in town**

Today I **sliced into a rat** to have a look inside
I gave some **poison to a cat** and watched him 'til he died
I **heated up some puppies** until their eyeballs fried
Then went home to my family, who **welcomed me with pride**

The government gives funding to the work we have to do
A necessary evil they say, **but that's not true**
They say **they're only animals,** not the same as me or you
So what's the point of all the TORTURE
that we put them through?

11   THE PRIDE
OF THE COUNTRYSIDE

Over-privileged hunters v brave saboteurs, it's very hard not to rhyme
hunt with cunt

The pride of the countryside

Look at us in our smart red coats how super do we look?
Riding round and chasing hounds *we just don't give a fuck*

> Look at you in your fancy pants going on your hunts
> Unhappy 'til you get a kill you *evil bunch of cunts*

Of course we force the horses to move the way they should
The dogs we train to hunt vermin and hunger for their blood

> The animals are just your tools they don't choose what they do
> And *if vermin truly were their goal they'd be chasing after you*

Tally Ho and off we go for another jolly ride
It doesn't matter what we do *the police are on our side*

> We know to you it's just a game and we're getting in your way
> But *this game has a victim*, so we'll sabotage your play

Keep off our land, you understand? Or we will mow you down
With bloody scars and smashed up cars you'll hobble back to town

> We'll mask the scent and blow our horns to distract your pack of hounds
> We're filming you and what you do, the *fox* remains unfound

We'll send our thugs to rough you up and take away your phones
You spoil our fun you'd better run or leave with broken bones

> You'll give up first so do your worst you *bloodthirsty violent scum*
> The police, it's true, will side with you but we're still gonna come

It's got too late, the *fox* can wait and die another day
The hounds have failed, our ship has sailed, the sabs have got their way

> If we'd won the day you'd be put away *what you're doing is a crime*
> But the law's too weak, your money speaks
> *so we'll see you here next time*

12   CAGED

Locked up for our amusement

Caged

My home is in a tiny cage and here's my tale of woe
I spread my wings and try to fly but there's *nowhere to go*
All I can do is hit the sides and flutter to-and-fro
And *scream for help* from all the people
come to *watch the show*
I should be free to fly away, soaring in the sky
To live in trees and other places safe for me, up high
Not locked in jail 'for my own good' until the day I die
How can they think I'm happy here? *I'm trapped inside a lie*

Here I sit in my own shit, watching from my cage
At people staring back at me, wanting me to rage
They call me a wild animal, *"ready to rampage"*
But they've turned me into just another sideshow on a stage
I should be free to roam the land, exploring every mile
Not stuck here for amusement and a random empty smile
With all the others just like me, *locked up without a trial*
Wasting away until the day we reach the 'useless' pile

We swim around in circles, looking for an out
People watching through the glass, laughing at our pout
Do they really think we have a life? Surely there's some doubt
*This isn't what the **meaning of existence** is about*
We should be free to swim whatever distance suits us best
In rivers, lakes and oceans, no limits east or west
To take our chance with bigger fish, a true survival test
Not bottled in captivity in a **cruel cold-blooded** jest

13   USED AND ABUSED

Animal abuse is everywhere, just let them live in peace

Used and Abused

Look at the **horses** on the racecourses, running as fast as they can
Given a say do you think that they would like to be *ridden by man?*
Maybe it's fun for them to run, but only when they choose
But when you force the poor horse, *that's nothing but abuse*

See the massive, very passive **elephants** over there
They're kept in chains and suffer pains by *people who don't care*
And then they're made, for tourist trade, to carry and amuse
It causes strife, this is no life, *it's nothing but abuse*

These overworked and very irked **donkeys** never stop
Every day the loads that they will *carry 'til they drop*
They're treated mean, as if machines, there's really no excuse
Then left to die, it makes me cry, *it's nothing but abuse*

We're at the **zoo**, I hope that you know what we're seeing here
They're all in jail, no chance of bail, and *sentenced every year*
Poached from the wild,
their lives defiled, for offspring they produce
And just so we can come and see, *that's nothing but abuse*

The 'dancing **bear**' is at the fair, some people think it's fun
She's getting laughs for photographs, *chained up so she can't run*
In the next cage the **monkey**'s rage is turning his face puce
And every day the tourists pay *for animal abuse*

The **orca** leaps, his big tail sweeps and rings the little bell
His joy is feigned, it's how he's trained in this, *his private Hell*
And all the while the **dolphin**'s smile *disguises her misuse*
They should be free to roam the sea, *what's that if not abuse?*

14   HORSE DISGRACE

More animal abuse, why the hell would they WANT another species to ride them?

HORSE disgRACE

I'm galloping *so fast, so fast, so fast* around the track
The little man is *whipping me* and *bouncing on my back*
I'm forced to run, it isn't fun for me and all my friends
So many jumps, *I just can't wait until this torture ends*

I seem to be a tool these humans use to play a game
If I win *they* take the credit, if I lose *I* take the blame
I'm leaking blood and sweat, *the straps are cutting up my skin*
The leech that's riding on my back assumes I want to win

But it's not my game, I'm only running fast *because I'm forced*
Expendable machinery these *man-beasts* call a horse
And thousands more are screaming out the names they make us wear
But it's not for us, *it's only for their money that they care*

I'm at the final hurdle, I'm so tired I could drop
But I'm in the lead so *no way that the horsewhipping will stop*
I've caught my foot, I'm going down, I've landed on my back
Something broke inside of me, I'm sure I felt it crack

I'm trying to get up again, he's shouting in my face
I'm on my feet, he leads me off, *ashamed at my disgrace*
It hurts to walk, the angry man is punching at my neck
We get inside, I wobble and collapse onto the deck

I wake to find another man looking down at me
He looks around then gets a gun from somewhere I can't see
Again he looks around and then he points it at my head
And this is where my story ends, I fear I may be dead

P G Holroyd

15 FISH FEEL PAIN

How could they not?

Fish Feel Pain

Imagine if some aliens invade your natural world
They snatch you up, by net or hook, and take you somewhere cold
Your lungs will heave, *you cannot breathe*, you're paralysed with fear
They take a knife to end your life, *you scream*, but they can't hear

This alien land, of air and sand is hostile to your kind
It feels so wrong, your friends are gone, you look but you can't find
You try to move, but in this world *your movement is diminished*
They bash your head, *again, again, again* until you're finished

These *monsters* from another world *don't care about your life*
You look so completely different, their contempt for you is rife
They don't understand your language, they can't hear your cries
They can't see *your fear* or the *terror in your eyes*

They think because you're different that *you don't feel any pain*
So they take you by the *billions* for their monetary gain
But you have a central nervous system, just the same as them
You have a brain, but they don't care, *you're a fish, and they are men*

You've heard before there's plenty *more fish out in the sea*
But if we carry on the way we are there isn't gonna be
And when they're gone it won't be long before the balance tips
And the world will feel the angry kiss of Mother Nature's lips

16   LIFE AFTER RESCUE

Please spare a thought for those unsung Heroes who dedicate their lives to look after rescued and disabled animals

Life After Rescue

Billions of animals all over the world, *born into slavery and
sentenced to death*
Regarded as products, to eat or to wear, their lives full of
terror *until their last breath*
Very few can escape this *nightmare on Earth*, there aren't
enough people who care for their plight
Just a handful of lucky ones rescued and saved, is that an
end to their story? *Well no, it's not quite*

Taken to *sanctuaries* run by people who care,
the first time in their lives they've experienced love
These unsung heroes dedicating their lives, *their
selflessness going beyond and above*
But there are limits, as always, to what they can do,
healthcare and housing, bedding and feed
These things don't come cheap, not to mention their time
They rely on donations to get what they need

Without thinking, *most people fund an animal's death*, very
few think that their life has some worth
If you're one of the few please help where you can, those
poor animals, *persecuted from birth*
Volunteer or donate, your *money* or your *time*, every
little bit matters, whatever it takes
It's not much to you but to them it's the world
And you'll feel *in your heart*
what a difference it makes

17   SANCTUARY SUPERHERO

Such hard work, no days off and sometimes heartbreaking, those animals are their family!

Sanctuary SUPERHERO

Here's a heartfelt tribute to all of you who run an animal
sanctuary or rescue
Dedicating your lives and giving your love so they have
bedding below, and shelter above
Often you go without food for yourself, you look after your
flock, but not your own health
Somehow providing whatever they need while struggling
to pay for their healthcare and feed

In all kinds of weather, however you feel,
the animals first, that's always the deal
Forever in wellies and covered in dirt, as long as they're
happy and nobody's hurt
And sometimes you have help, but mostly alone, working
late in the evening 'til everything's done
Wondering if anyone cares what you do, *worried* what
would happen to them without you

So if you feel down when nobody's there please know that
we see you, *know that we care*
To us you're a *hero*, a huge force for good, doing what
most of us only dream that we could
Most farm animals in this world are *living in Hell* but you
give them a *Heaven*, and treat them so well
Be proud of yourself and all that you do, from the bottom of
our hearts, we say a massive *THANKYOU*

18   DID I MENTION I'M VEGAN?

As the joke goes" How can you tell when somebody's vegan?
Don't worry, they'll tell you". Here's why...

Did I mention I'm Vegan?

The reason I told you *I'm vegan*
When you asked what I wanted to eat
Is so I don't get remains of *someone with brains*
On my plate in the form of meat

The reason I tell you *I'm vegan*
When you offer me something to drink
Is because I try to refrain from causing the pain
Of *an animal able to think*

The reason I say that *I'm vegan*
When I'm looking for something to wear
Is so I don't end up in a *poor animal's skin*
Because I'm one of those people who care

The reason I shout that *I'm vegan*
When I'm standing alone in the crowd
Is so people will see that someone like me
Is *happy to say it out loud*

The reason my clothes say *I'm vegan*
When I'm protesting for a good cause
Is to let people know that I'm ready to go
All the way to *change outdated laws*

The reason *I'm proud to be vegan*
Even though a minority still
Is that now I'm awake *for the animals sake*
And not helping the industries kill

19   I WANT A VEGAN

Much better to have a partner with equal ethics, but not always possible

I Want a Vegan

I want to date a vegan, no one else will do

I need to know our ***principles*** are bonded like a glue

I won't go near a meat-eater, don't care how good they look

The things they eat and what they wear make them an
ugly fuck

Don't want a *vegetarian,* they're not the same as me

They still support the ***awful eggs and dairy industry***

It has to be a ***vegan partner***, if it's going to last

I know this from experience, I'm learning from my past

But if I never find one who wants to be with me

*I'll settle for some **vegan cake** and a **nice cup of tea***

20   THE 'V' WORD
Guess what 'V' stands for

The 'V' Word

Don't say *the 'v' word*, it puts some people off
They act as if you swore or spat a word out with a cough
They hear that word and straight away
you see them start to tense
They think you are attacking so they go on the defence
If you say *the 'v' word*, get ready to be schooled
About your health and how your diet choices have you fooled
They'll talk about tradition and the normal way to live
How animals are happy with the lives they *want* to give

Don't say *the 'v' word*, use another word instead
You wouldn't want to make them
think about the way they're fed
You can say you're *vegetarian*, that seems to be okay
But shorten that to *vegan* and you'll see them run away
Plant-based describes the food you eat but
not the life you live
Being *vegan is a lifestyle, there's no other word to give*
They think it's too extreme that we care about all life
**But it's fine to fund the violence of the
bloody butcher's knife**

Don't say *the 'v' word*, unless you want a fight
It's hard for them to understand that **they might not be right**
If you use *the 'v' word* you'd better know your stuff
It doesn't matter what you say, for them it's not enough
It's such a massive change to make,
they think inside their head
Much easier not to change at all and keep eating the dead
So if you say *the 'v' word*, make sure you say it loud
Because if you are a **VEGAN** then
you should be fucking proud!

21 WHY AM I VEGAN?

Vegan means you care about animals, why would anybody
question that?

Why am I Vegan?

Do you know what you're saying when you ask
why I'm vegan?

Do I really have to spell it out?

You're asking why I don't support *animal abuse*

Because that's what it's really about

To be vegan means *we don't eat their flesh*

Or anything that they produce

We don't wear their skin or *use them as tools*

Do we need another excuse?

To be vegan means that we *care for all life*

And *respect* the existence they've got

So the next time you think about asking that question

Maybe ask yourself why you're not

22   SO, YOU'RE A CARNIVORE?

A carnivore is an animal that ONLY eats the flesh of other animals

So, you're a *CARNIVORE*?

So, you tell me you're a CARNIVORE
That's funny 'cause I thought I saw
You eating fruit and veg before
When I came through the door

Anatomically we're HERBIVORE
That's what our bodies hunger for
Although it's true we've eaten more
A fact we can't ignore

That's why they call us OMNIVORE
Because of meat we ate before
But we don't need that anymore
These aren't the days of yore

In fact, if we were CARNIVORE, we'd **make a kill** and
eat it raw, and **lick the blood** up off the floor, and
kill a rabbit with our **claw**, and sink our **face in all the
gore**, and hunger for a **bone to gnaw**, and **chase a scent** we
can't ignore, and really **want to kill** some more, and bellow
out a **massive roar**,
but we don't do that anymore,
we feed on plants and beans galore, 'cause naturally we're
HERBIVORE,
we get our **dinner from the store**, and **keep it in the freezer**
drawer, so that's why, as I've said before,
there's no way you're a CARNIVORE!

23   VEGAN FOOD

Pretty much everything edible that doesn't come from an animal,
it's just food

Vegan Food

I don't mean to be rude but the things in your food make it inedible
The things you eat each time we meet are just incredible
There's **blood and gore** and so much more, the whole thing *stinks of death*
Yet still you eat and think it's sweet, it makes me catch my breath
You think it's fresh that *piece of flesh* that used to have a life
You think it's good that *taste of blood* that oozes from your knife
But in the end you'll see my friend the nutrients they lack
Cholesterol and heart disease will move in to attack

You think my food is weird because it *didn't need to kill*
You say you couldn't eat it, that it's *gonna make me ill*
You call it *"vegan food"* as if it's from another world
But *it's just food without the body parts if truth were to be told*
There's nothing added to my food to make it *veganised*
It's what's left out that matters as you should have realised
Vegetables, fruits and other **plants**, things you already eat
So why cause pain and suffering to get milk, eggs and meat

In olden days we followed ways our ancestors began
We couldn't find alternatives, *but nowadays we can*
The **plants** and **grains** and **beans** we eat are *perfect for our health*
But businesses have spent too much and want to keep their wealth
As vegans we have everything, *we eat just what we please*
From **sausage rolls** to **pizza**, and from **chocolates** to **cheese**
No need to kill an animal to get the foods we need
It's amazing all the flavours stemming from a humble seed

The vegan movement grows, and it gets bigger every day
It's easier than you think to live your life a different way
It's all about *compassion* and *respecting* life on Earth
Not just our own but *every life* entitles equal worth
So when you think of **vegan food**, remember it's not weird
It's more natural than your *'murder on a plate'* at first appeared
As more people change, the more the range of choices in the shops
And hopefully, one day, *will be the day the killing stops*

24 WHERE DO YOU GET YOUR PROTEIN?

A common argument aimed at vegans, we manage

Where do you get your protein?

Where do you get your protein?
The lion asked the giraffe

*It's obvious, from the plants I eat, are you
having a laugh?*

Where do you get your protein?
The tiger asked the cow

*I get it from the plants,
the only way that I know how*

Where do you get your protein?
The hyena asked the deer

There's plenty in the plants I eat,
he answered with a jeer

Where do you get your protein?
Someone asked the vegan

I get it from my food you pillock!
Said the vegan

25 THE VEGAN DILEMMA

Lots of vegans face this dilemma with their families, stay strong, it's good to be different

The **VEGAN** Dilemma

It's that time again, we're going out for a
three-course family meal
As I'm the only vegan no one considers how I feel
The restaurants booked, I've had a look,
there's not much I can eat
I'm told *"cheer up"* I'm *lucky* I'm included in this *treat*
I've got two Nans, they always tell me *not to make a fuss*
Dad says I'm the only *troublemaker* out of all of us
My uncle say he understands the arguments I'm picking
But for just this one occasion *can't I settle for the chicken*

I'd rather stay at home but then I'm ruining their big day
I'm being selfish if I spoil the family meal in any way
My starter is a **salad** with a **dry unbuttered roll**
The main a plate of **vegetables** and **wedges** in a bowl
My cousins keep on taunting me with *little strips of meat*
The worst part is to look at all the *awful things they eat*
At least it's nearly over, as the puddings are en route
I'm asked if I've enjoyed so I just *smile* and eat my **fruit**

Next time I'll have to stand my ground and just refuse to go
I love them, but they should recognise the reasons I say *no*
I'll make my point, it's all *about the animals*, not them
I don't want to contribute to actions I condemn
I'll find some friends like me and maybe we can
take the pledge
So we can only eat with other people who eat **veg**
And hopefully one day my family will understand
When vegan options grow enough to satisfy demand

26   HAPPY EASTER

Not much to celebrate, but the bank holiday's a bonus

Happy Easter

Do you celebrate Easter because some bloke long ago
According to the *hearsay*
Was murdered on Friday, got up on the Sunday
And then he just went on his way
Leaving behind him **confusion and chaos**
And a nice weekend bank holiday

Do you celebrate Easter for the chocolate eggs?
Made with the *milk from a cow*
Stolen from mothers with babies to feed
Do you think that they celebrate now?
While you stuff your face *they cry for their mums*
Are you proud of yourself? Take a bow!

Do you celebrate Easter with a nice *leg of lamb?*
Smothered in gravy and sauce
That lamb was born just a few months ago
Taken from their mother *by force*
You're eating a baby who wanted to live
But you don't care about that of course

I don't celebrate Easter for all the above
But I'm happy to take the days off
I have plenty to eat without *suffering and death*
Lots of plant-based chocolates to scoff
And **I celebrate life** that all species deserve
Not the **death** that you eat from your trough

27   MOTHER'S DAY

The arrogance of humans, thinking we're the only species that loves their children

Mother's Day

It's *Mother's Day*, so time to say *"I love you"* to your Mum, though
every day would be ok to get that duty done
She's had a say in every way, the person you've become, still here
today, or gone away, *you're lucky you had one*
Although it's true for some of you *the love may not be there*, if she
withdrew, abandoned you or simply didn't care
But you got through, as people do when life becomes unfair, so this is
you, the person who can make it anywhere

Though *not all mums are human, every species is the same,*
they all gave birth and felt the worth as their new baby came
Too many times they face the crimes of *theft by human hands,* their
babies gone they're left alone, it's hard to understand
For years they've been *breeding machines,* used up and thrown away, in
the name of profit gain, *it's animals who pay*
They cause them strife then *take their life,* as long as there's demand,
the *sentient souls who pay the tolls* and end up as a brand

So spare a thought, as we all ought, for *captive motherhood,* the ones
distraught whose lives are fraught with misery in mud
Their milk is bought, their **babies** brought to *slavery and blood,*
reduced to nought, their futures caught in lives misunderstood
A callous deed, they're forced to breed, just for financial gain, because
of greed they take their seed through *suffering and pain*
The more you read the less your need to ride this gravy train, don't
make them bleed *we all can feed in ways much more humane*

An awful fate, a constant state of *enforced pregnancy,* behind a gate
without a mate, a *breeding factory*
To desolate and separate from early infancy, and then to wait inside a
crate in a *cold laboratory*
A mother is a mother, the species matters not, a human or another,
it's just one life we've got
It breaks the heart, please don't take part, it doesn't take a lot, just
don't buy from their businesses and watch their profits rot!

28   MORE THAN A NUMBER

Billions of them, each one an individual

More than a number

In another life, a better life, this **cow** would have a name
She'd be surrounded by loved ones and feel alive
But in this life, of pain and strife she's no more than a number
A milk machine marked *one three seven five* **1375**

This **sheep** is full of *meat* and *wool* and numbered *eighty-six*
That's all she's for and nothing more they say
But *she should be free* and full of glee with all the other sheep
Not giving all her property away **86**

These **lambs** so young and full of fun should have a life to live
But it's *Easter* now so soon they will be gone
Without a name they're all the same, *killed and cooked for dinner*
Just numbered from *fifteen to fifty-one* **15-51**

Just take a look inside this truck, there's one of many **pigs**
He had no chance of ever being free
It's such a waste, he'll be the taste of breakfast or a sandwich
His ear tag reads *two hundred twenty-three* **223**

This **rabbit** here is feeling queer inside his little cage
He's been injected every day with *human flu*
He lost his sight the other night from *tests involving bleach*
He's only known as subject *twenty-two* **22**

The **greyhound**'s pace will win the race, his coat says number *one*
A tidy profit for his ownership
But all the same, when he goes lame and starts to lag behind
He'll be *discarded and dumped* inside a skip **1**

Same time, same day but miles away **five different species** die
Along with all their family and friends
Cow, pig, goat, sheep and **dog**, one number links them all
Numbers *'ninety-seven'* meet their gruesome ends **97**

29 THE VIOLENCE OF THE LAMBS

It's amazing, people see lambs in the field and go all gooey, then sit down to eat them.

The Violence of the Lambs

Beautiful babies, taken from their mothers

Thrown onto lorries with hundreds of others

Nullified and terrified, they make the trip in silence

Heading for the *slaughterhouse,* a
world of pain and violence

Beautiful babies murdered for a meal

Legs cut off and sold as a 2 for 1 deal

Lambs and mothers lose, but
hey, you're a winner

Because that's what you pay for
when you buy your Sunday dinner

30   WHAT IF ... {IT WAS US}?

Put yourself in their shoes, I don't think you'd like it! This is happening to other beings, it's not fiction.

What if ... [it was us]?

What if all those years ago *we didn't win the race*
And another stronger species evolved to take our place
They had the skills, they had the brains to dominate us all
We didn't get the chance to grow, *we had no chance at all*
They learned to build, they liked to kill, and *humans were their prey*
They *hunted* us, they *tasted* us, *we couldn't get away*
They ate our flesh while we were fresh, *they even wore our skin*
They took our seed and *made us breed* whilst *murdering our kin*

As time went on they grew more strong and we remained the weak
We had no choice, **we had no voice**, *they bred us to be meek*
Terrified and *broken* we did as we were told
For *we were only children*, had no chance of growing old
So good was our taste they left no waste, they used up every bit
Our hair made silk, *our mothers' milk was taken from the tit*
They had their fun, they made us run, their children rode our backs
They cut us wide to look inside and hung us up on racks

Once we're grown, though still so young we're taken on the road
With *prodding sticks* and *vicious kicks* we're forced to join the load
From a life in chains the **hope remains** that *we might be set free*
We didn't know that we would go and meet our *destiny*
Now off the truck and just one look is all that we will need
The smell of fear, the sounds we hear from children in the lead
We wait in line, now it's our time, they *hit us on the head*
Our throats are cut, they hang us up and *leave us 'til we're dead*

Now they farm us by the *billions*, the whole world demands our *meat*
We're *killed in such large numbers*, so much more than they can eat
They feed us on the plants that should be fed to their own kind
In the starving third world countries that have all been left behind
The land they use for our abuse is *killing off the world*
Yet still they **breed and murder** all the human boys and girls
We won't be free until they see the error of their ways
Or failing that, *the planet cracks and takes us all away*

31　THE TRUTH

Just because you don't want to believe it,
doesn't mean it's not true

The Truth

We're standing on a street in the middle of a town

Showing covert footage of the *truth*

Hoping to, one day, bring the slaughterhouses down

By letting people stop and see the *proof*

We let them know the *consequences* of the food they buy

That factory farming's terrible and cruel

They're paying for the suffering of *babies who will die*

I can't believe they don't teach this in school

To some it makes a difference, but others just don't care

Ignoring us and trying to stay aloof

But we will keep on trying to make them all aware

That the things we say and show them are the *TRUTH*

32   ANIMAL ACTIVIST

People who have the guts to stand up for what they believe in

Animal Activist

When someone takes a job hurting animals
In a **slaughterhouse**, a **lab** or a **farm**
Nobody cares, *"a job is a job"*
Never mind that you're causing them harm
But when somebody tries to protest
And stands up for the animals' rights
People get mad, they call them *a freak*
And say they just like causing fights

Society says that to *torture and kill*
Is accepted for **research** or **food**
But to dare to object, and want to protect
Just makes us *obnoxious* and *rude*
So we try to be heard as we stand in the street
And that makes us an activist
If we get in the way, to rescue or save
Then they call us a terrorist

Most people would say they *love animals*
In between eating mouthfuls of **flesh**
What they really mean is their *cat* or their *dog*
Not the ones described *'free-range'* or *'fresh'*
But *there's no difference*, **they all want to live**
We should, all of us, care for their plights
They can't speak for themselves, so *we give them a voice*
Get active, for animal rights

33   REASONS NOT TO BE VEGAN

Some of the most common excuses, when really, they just don't
want to because they don't care enough

Reasons not to be Vegan

You say you eat meat because it's *what we've always done*
Why change an *old tradition* we've had since time begun?
Well, we also *invaded countries* and took them off as *slaves*
We *murdered, raped* and *pillaged,* we used to live in caves
If we kept on doing all the things we always used to do
We'd be *racist, sexist monsters,* **am I describing you?**

You say your *teeth are canine,* that they're made for *eating meat*
You say that only *animal protein* makes your meal complete
But I bet you couldn't catch a deer and *kill her with your teeth*
And **plants** and **beans** and **nuts** provide your protein without grief
You say a *lion kills animals* to eat, so why can't you?
But a lion doesn't have the choice to join the checkout queue

You say that *God made animals for us to use and kill*
That every other species is *subject to our will*
But the only way you'd know what your God did or what He said
Is because you made Him up, *He only lives inside your head*
And even if He did exist and lived up to His fame
He'd take one look at what we've done and *run away in shame*

So when you say that you can't live a *vegan lifestyle*
You're really saying **you don't care which species you defile**
But every single time you buy your **meat,** your **milk,** your **eggs**
You're paying for someone to be *killed and hung up by their legs*
And if you realise the truth but still you just don't care
Then *you're not deserving* of that
costume of compassion that you wear

34   WOKEN FROM THE MATRIX

A reference to the film where people were being factory farmed by
machines and their 'real world' was all in their mind

WOKEN from the MATRIX

Your life before awakening was *ignorant and bliss*
You thought that *vegan activists* were just taking the piss
That *'loving animals'* meant *give your favourite pet a kiss*
But *now you know the truth* about all this

If you choose the **red**, it's a bitter pill to swallow
To *speak up for the voiceless* is the path you have to follow
If you choose the **blue**, return to apathy and hollow
It's in the blood of innocents you wallow

Now that you're awake the real *nightmare* can begin
It feels like it's a battle that we're never gonna win
You're going to get abuse, you'll have to *take it on the chin*
So now you need to *grow a thicker skin*

The **MATRIX** is society, *filling us with lies*
Feeding us the carcasses of everyone who dies
Acting like they're angels, but they're **devils in disguise**
Now we see through them, with open eyes

No longer will we fall for their *evil little tricks*
Their façade is collapsing, there's nothing left to fix
We'll build a better future, *using truth as bricks*
We've woken up, outside of the **Matrix**

35 EARTHLINGS

Earthlings, someone born and living on the Planet Earth,
regardless of species.

*Earth*lings

When you think of an *Earthling* what do you see?

Do you only see people like *you and me*?

We're just a small fraction of creatures on **Earth**

We all have a life, we all have some worth

We all have the instincts to *try to survive*

We all have the right to *keep loved ones alive*

So, live and let live, *no one has to die*

We're all Earthlings together, give vegan a try

P G Holroyd

FOR THE ANIMALS

P G Holroyd

Printed in Great Britain
by Amazon